THE WORST OF THE VIKINGS

Margaret McAllister

Illustrated by Scoular Anderson

This book is for all my friends from Viking lands,
including all the Scandinavians who came to Alnwick
Music Festival. Especially, my love and thanks go to
the Synnes and Mollestad families.

PACIFIC
L E A R N I N G

© 2001 Pacific Learning
© 2000 Written by **Margaret McAllister**
Illustrated by **Scoular Anderson**
US Edit by **Rebecca Weber McEwen**

This Americanized Edition of *The Worst of the Vikings*,
originally published in English in 2000, is published
by arrangement with Oxford University Press.

05 04 03 02 01
10 9 8 7 6 5 4 3 2 1

Published by
Pacific Learning
P.O. Box 2723
Huntington Beach, CA 92647-0723
www.pacificlearning.com

ISBN: 1-59055-054-4
PL-7503

Contents

Very
Cold

Home
of the
Vikings

Northumberland
(England)

End of the
World

Edwinsbay

Boat
Cave

Ingy's Bay

Dunes

CHAPTER 1

The Anger of Harald Hairyhand

By the late white sun of a winter afternoon, three Viking warriors gazed across the sea. Tangled hair stuck out wildly from beneath their helmets. Behind them, on the cliff top, bitter black smoke filled the sky.

Were they gazing in triumph toward their homeland?

No. Not these three. They were in disgrace.

The tallest, whose name was Torpid, was almost asleep. The others who were, in order of height, Vapid and Morbid, were wondering what would happen when the Viking leader caught up with them.

To tell you how they came to be in trouble, we have to go back to the early morning, when their longships were speeding across the sea.

In the prow of the leading ship stood their chief. His hair and beard were fair as a cornfield, his blue eyes were fierce, and his sword was in his hand. He was Harald Hairyhand. He was leading his men across the North Sea to raid villages, take the animals, and carry great riches home to Norway.

At one time, men used to call him Harald Stubbylegs because he was the only Viking who had to stand on tiptoe to kiss his granny. Luckily, he'd grown into a powerful fighter. The last man to call him "Harald Stubbylegs" never spoke again. (Though he does still hum the tunes of his favorite childhood songs, but that's what being *really* scared can do to a person.) Now he was the great Harald Hairyhand. From his yellow hair and beard to the toes of his enormous boots, (he wore very thick boots to make himself taller), he was feared more than all other Vikings – except one.

The sweating fair-haired men pulling the oars could see a beach and a cliff top, with a huddle of small wooden buildings. Goats, sheep, and cattle grazed nearby.

"Looks sort of nice, doesn't it?" said Vapid.

"Stop your noise at the back of the boat, or I'll feed you to the fish!" Harald roared. "When we reach the shore, we climb up to the village quickly and quietly. Take them by surprise because anyone you meet will run before you to try to warn the others. Drive the animals down to the beach. Steal anything that's worth having."

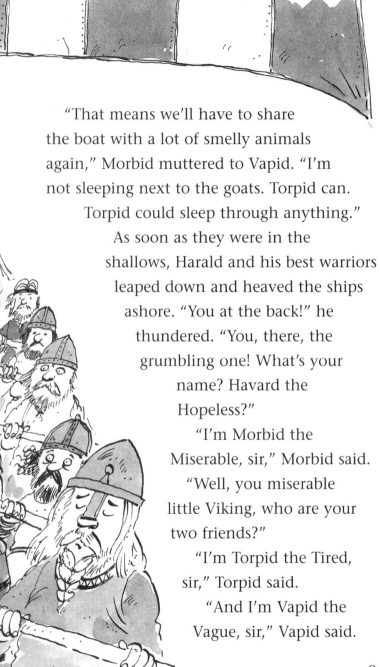

"That means we'll have to share
the boat with a lot of smelly animals
again," Morbid muttered to Vapid. "I'm
not sleeping next to the goats. Torpid can.
Torpid could sleep through anything."

As soon as they were in the
shallows, Harald and his best warriors
leaped down and heaved the ships
ashore. "You at the back!" he
thundered. "You, there, the
grumbling one! What's your
name? Havard the
Hopeless?"

"I'm Morbid the
Miserable, sir," Morbid said.

"Well, you miserable
little Viking, who are your
two friends?"

"I'm Torpid the Tired,
sir," Torpid said.

"And I'm Vapid the
Vague, sir," Vapid said.

"Oh," said Harald, "the dozy one and the dippy one. You three take the quickest path up the cliffs – the path to the left, can you see it, you idiots? That means you'll get to the town first, you lucky Vikings! So if anyone is left guarding that end of this pathetic village, who is in trouble?"

"We are, sir," said Morbid.

"Now, Vikings," Harald roared, "follow me! Fire! Plunder! Pillage!"

Morbid, Torpid, and Vapid trudged up the path. The other warriors ran for the steeper, slower climb up the cliffs.

"I hate plundering," Morbid said. "I'd rather be on deck-scrubbing duty, but I always get plundering."

"I'm too tired to pillage," Torpid yawned. "All that rowing wears you out."

"I've never been quite sure what *pillage* means," Vapid said. "It's sort of stealing, isn't it? We'll be in trouble if we don't join in. We'd better just pillage a little bit."

Nobody was guarding the village. Torpid, Vapid, and Morbid looked around and wondered how they could plunder and pillage without causing too much trouble.

The other Vikings were still swarming up the cliffs with drawn swords when Vapid saw a brown-and-white goat grazing nearby. A loose rope was around its neck.

"I suppose we could sort of steal the goat," he suggested. "Is that pillaging?"

"It'll bite," Morbid warned.

The Viking warriors had arrived in the village now, roaring with the rage of battle. The villagers screamed and ran and the animals stampeded, horses whinnying in distress.

"Move yourselves, or I'll see that you pay!" Harald roared as he ran past.

"We'd better get out of his way," Morbid said. "Is there anywhere safe?"

They were near the largest building in the village, which was the only one made of stone. At least it wouldn't burn down.

They slipped inside, Vapid leading the goat. Torpid shut the door to keep the noise out.

"It's dark," Morbid said. "I can't see if there's anything worth plundering."

As their eyes became used to the darkness, they could make out a cross-shaped thing gleaming at the other end of the building, and something in front of it. It might have been a small treasure box.

"At least there's nobody here, so we won't have to bother anyone," Torpid said. "What about that cross-shaped thing – is it gold? We could plunder that, if it isn't too heavy."

"I'm interested in the thing that looks like a box," Vapid said. "Look at this flat and square-ish thing. What is it?"

Morbid pulled the brightly painted thing toward him. Something gleamed in the dark.

"Jewels!" Torpid said. "Careful how you lift it up, it's falling apart."

"Typical," Morbid grumbled. "Stuff always falls apart for me." But what looked to him like a box falling apart was, in fact, a book.

Morbid had heard of books, but had never seen one. He carried it to a tiny window and turned the pages very, very carefully, because he was afraid of breaking something.

None of them spoke. Nothing they had seen, on sea, on land, in battle, or at peace, had prepared them for anything so wonderful. They had not dreamed of such patterns, such colors, such delicate twists of scarlet and purple, blue and gold. They gazed at the book as if they were soaking up its color and craftsmanship. The gold edgings and the neat rows of black patterns must surely mean something, if only they understood it.

In the margins were skillful drawings of birds with long, intertwined bodies and fierce beaks. There was a cat and a lion and an eagle. Swirls, circles, and spirals, curls and whirls, were so bright that the colors could have been alive and singing.

CLANG CLASH DING

The pealing of a bell crashed through the silence. They jumped, shrieked, and reached for their swords, wildly looking around, up and down. Where was the enemy?

"It's the stupid goat!" Morbid growled.

The goat had wandered off and found the bell rope. He was chewing hard at it with determined little tugs. By the time the three of them had hauled the bell rope from the goat and the goat from the bell rope, the clanging was deafening.

When it stopped, they heard shouts, the blowing of horns, and the clash of weapons rapidly growing louder and louder. Every person for miles around must have heard that bell.

"Oops," Morbid said. "We've woken up the opposition."

"I don't think we should have done that," Vapid said.

"Sometimes, it's best not to wake up in the mornings at all," Torpid sighed. "Now what do we do?"

"Er… I guess we could… sort of…" Vapid began nervously.

"Pillage and run?" Morbid said. He stuffed the book down the front of his tunic, and they grabbed as many of the gold pieces as they could carry.

"That'll do," Torpid said, who thought that the real trouble with plundering was carrying all that heavy plunder back to the longships. "Let's see if we can get this down to the beach without running into anyone."

They scurried to the door, Vapid
leading the goat. Morbid gave
the church door a hefty
shove and tripped over his
feet as it was opened from
outside by a strong hand.

It was a hairy hand. Harald's hairy hand,
that is, holding his battle-ax.

"I've come to chop the rope to that blasted
bell. If I find who rang it, I'll make the slob
clean the barnacles off the boat with his
teeth! The whole countryside is streaming in
to help this village! Who rang that bell?"
he roared.

Morbid grumbled and Torpid shuffled and they both stammered that it had nothing to do with them.

They might have gotten away with it if Vapid hadn't appeared at that moment with the goat, which had a section of the rope still dangling from his mouth. The Vikings, stuttering and trembling as they handed over the cross and candlesticks, were terrified of Harald, but the goat wasn't. It just stared at him, chewing steadily at a tassel.

"That's a *bell* rope!" Harald roared, as he tightened his grip on his battle-ax.

"No, it's just any old rope," Vapid dithered. With the side of his ax, Harald whomped the bottom of each Viking in turn.

"You – hopeless – imbeciles!" he yelled, with a wallop for every word. "Get back to the boats and stay there, and take that goat! Oh, and," he called after them as they ran, clutching their bottoms, for the shore, "after all this, I might just peg you down on the beach and leave you for the crows!"

They ran from the village, where armed
men who had heard the ringing of the bell
were charging in from every side to fight off
the Vikings. Hand to hand and sword to
sword they struggled as Torpid, Vapid, and
Morbid ran to the beach. They looked out to
sea. Home was a long way away.

"Will he really feed us to the crows?"
Morbid asked. "He's angry enough."

They tried to think of a way of escaping,
and Vapid suggested stealing a longship, but
Morbid pointed out that it took a whole crew
of Vikings to row one.

"He can't leave us to the crows," said
Vapid. "There aren't any. There are only
those little fat things that waddle around."

"Babies?" Torpid said.

"No, puffins," Vapid said. "They look
friendly. I don't suppose they'll eat us, if they
really are friendly."

"They will if they're hungry," Morbid said. "With our luck they will be." Then nobody said anything until it started to rain.

They looked nervously at each other, then over their shoulders. At that moment, Harald Hairyhand was too busy fighting to notice if they disobeyed orders.

They shuffled along the beach and, because the tide was out, were able to walk around the jutting cliffs to a sheltered little bay. There was a cave there, cold and dark, but at least it was dry. Huddling inside, they all saw the same thing.

A boat! It was small enough to row, but big enough to carry them all. It had been left at the back of the cave, with the oars in it.

"Nice boat," Torpid said.

"It would be a nice bit of pillage," Vapid said. "Stealing a boat is kind of pillaging, isn't it?"

"Not if we steal it for ourselves," Morbid said. "It's only pillaging if we steal it for Harald." They all knew that they had no intention of handing over anything to Harald – certainly not a boat. They decided not to hand in themselves, either. Together they pushed the boat to the water's edge.

"Can we keep the goat?" Vapid asked. "It might be useful, you know. It seems like a nice goat too."

However the goat did not want to get into the boat. They pushed it and pulled it, but it stood still. They picked it up and stood it in the boat, and it climbed out again. They tried one more time. It kicked Morbid, butted Torpid, and ran away.

"Jump in," Torpid said. "We'll have to go without it."

"I always get wetter than anyone else," Morbid grumbled as they pushed the boat into the water and climbed in. They saw the goat trotting carelessly across the sand – then a bellow thundered through the air.

"HEY! You there in the boat!
Where do you think you're going?"
"That wasn't the goat talking,
was it?" Vapid asked.
Above them, on a cliff top,
Harald Hairyhand stood like
a figurehead. He shook his
spear and started racing
down the cliff after
them. The Vikings slunk
down, hoping he wouldn't recognize them.
As Harald ran, he tripped on a loose stone
and crashed to the ground. His spear flew out
of his hand and into the water.
Morbid fished it out.

"May as well keep it," he said. "I don't suppose it'll be of any use, but it's a pity to just let it sink. Now, where are we going?"

"To sleep," Torpid said, and did.

"Let's go thataway," Vapid said, pointing away from the burning village. He didn't really care where they went, so long as it was away from Harald.

"Yes, but where's 'thataway'? Where's the nearest land?"

"Um… um… er… Morbid, do you know these waters at all?"

There was no sound but the slosh of the oars. Then Morbid said, "You don't know where we're going, do you?"

"Sort of – well, no. Do you?"

Dip, slosh, went the oars. Dip, slosh.

"I don't suppose we have any food or fresh water," Morbid said.

After digging in their leather pouches they found dry bread, a drinking pouch half full of water, and a piece of very hard cheese. It had been there a long time, and smelled of feet.

"That should keep us going for... er..."
Vapid said hesitantly.

"Not very long," Morbid said.

Torpid lay on a hillside in the sunshine, with music playing nearby. The harvest was in, and beautiful Viking girls sat whispering together happily. Then the prettiest of them, with flowers in her hair, picked up a jug of cool water and walked toward him, smiling. She held out the jug and... emptied it over him.

Torpid woke from his dream and leaped
to his feet.

"I'm soaked!" he yelled. Then the boat
rocked, and he remembered where he was.
"This stupid boat leaks!"

CHAPTER 2

Lost in the Mist

"We should have known," Morbid grumbled. He took off his helmet and jammed it into the leak. "That's why this boat was left alone in that cave with its oars. It needed to be repaired. Hand over your tunic, Vapid, it's leaking around the edge of my helmet."

"So why does it have to be *my* tunic?" Vapid asked irritably.

"It won't help," Torpid yawned. "It'll be soaked through in no time. Why don't you use Harald's spear?"

They plugged the leak by ramming the spear point into the hole. There was still a small puddle seeping very slowly around it, but they bailed that out with their helmets.

It grew dark. They took turns holding the spear in the hole and bailing out. They ate and drank a little of their rations, then decided that they had to make the food last.

They put the rest away, but pulled it out again a few minutes later and ate a bit more. They took turns keeping watch through the night, and even Torpid agreed to stay awake for as long as he could – but after a day and a night, when the food was finished and the water nearly gone, they were all asleep.

Vapid woke, shivering, stiff, and very cold. He stood up, swaying with the movement of the boat. It was still dark but he could see the water was shallow, so he stepped out and pulled the boat up the beach as far as he could. He wanted to wake the others and tell them they'd reached land, but they had been so tired, and were so fast asleep, that he left them. From the rising of the sun behind him, he knew he was facing west. (He should have figured out that he was in the same country as before – just farther down the coast – but he'd never been clear about directions.)

He was clear about something else, though. He was hungry, and there wasn't a thing in sight to eat.

High cliffs and sand dunes were all around, and he saw winding paths that led through the dunes and a narrow pass through the cliffs. Taking the spear, he headed for the right path, changed his mind and turned left, then thought again and headed for the middle, straight across the sand dunes.

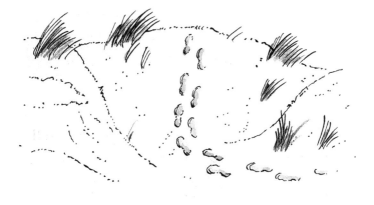

If he had thought of the dangers of exploring a strange place alone, he wouldn't have done it, but in his hurry to find something to eat he was soon over the dunes and out of sight of the beach.

The sun was rising as Morbid sat up and saw that they had beached. He kicked Torpid to wake him up, and kicked him again to *really* wake him up, because he'd gone right back to sleep.

"Vapid's gone," Morbid said, looking around. "He's bound to get lost, so we'll have to find him. We'll probably get eaten by wild animals or taken prisoner, but I suppose we should try. You take the right path through the sand dunes, and I'll go by the cliffs on the left. I'll meet you back here when the sun's overhead. Got it?"

Torpid yawned and stumbled to the sand dunes. He started singing to wake himself up, and because he liked singing. Morbid stomped off to the cliffs.

By the time the sun was overhead, Torpid had stopped for a rest and fallen asleep again, and Morbid was lost.

The mist was swirling in from the sea, wrapping a thin gray cloud around Vapid as he walked farther and farther over the dunes and down into a valley. The mist reached the valley before him, and the more he walked, the more he sank into its gray folds. He could see only a few yards ahead, and then hardly at all.

"Never mind," he thought, "I never knew where I was going in the first place, so I'm no worse off." Then he heard a woman scream.

He reached for his sword, couldn't find it, and remembered Harald's spear. Spear in hand he ran toward the scream, knowing that he should shout something, although he wasn't sure what. Then he remembered how Harald used to shout, "Plunder! Pillage!" and he yelled it with all his strength.

Dimly he could see a shape ahead of him, becoming clearer with every step. There was a woman, in a homespun tunic that was splattered with something red – it was on her hands, and on the cauldron in front of her.

It even dripped from the hefty stick she held in both hands. She glared with rage.

"Come one step closer and I'll do the plundering and the pillaging!" she snarled as she brandished the reddened stick.

"Oh – sorry." Vapid backed away. "Um, good morning – um – I thought you screamed. I was coming to help. Well, since it appears you're all right, I'll go. It was nice meeting you."

"Oh, don't worry about the scream, my dear," she said. She smiled, put down the stick, and rubbed her red hands on her tunic. "I just lost my temper with this useless dye, and when I dropped the cauldron on my foot, I let out a good old-fashioned bellow."

"Oh!" Vapid said. "Dye?"

"Yes, dye," she said. "I make a lot of that. Dye for cloth and paint for decoration and books and things like that. Come here, if you like, and if you promise not to do any pillaging and plundering."

Morbid went on trudging between the cliffs.
He, too, was hampered by the mist.

"I may as well keep going," he muttered.
"I'll probably find armies on one side,
dragons on the other, and a sheer drop in
front of me, but I may as well go on."

So he went on, and walked into a wall.

He staggered back, muttering to himself as his brain spun inside his head. As the dizziness cleared and his eyes stopped watering, he heard a voice.

"Narrow is the gate, and few are those that find it. You missed, brother. Come this way."

Hand on his battle-ax, he followed the voice and walked into a smoky darkness that made him blink and scrunch his eyes until he became used to it. The smoke came from a small fire of sticks and sea coal, and by its glow he saw an old man with a white beard.

"Blessings to you," the old man said. Morbid didn't know what that meant, but the old man spoke gently and carried no weapons, so he supposed it wasn't anything unpleasant. He crouched to warm himself over the fire, and the old man brought him bread and water. Morbid gladly ate, keeping his hand on his battle-ax, and watching the firelight dancing on the walls.

There were patterns on those walls, and they reminded him of something.

He went to look more closely, tracing the shapes with his finger. The feeling that he was being watched made him turn, and he saw the old man behind him.

"What do all of these squiggles mean?" Morbid asked.

Far away, Torpid woke up in a shady forest. From somewhere came music and Torpid sat up, wide awake and listening.

The music stopped. A voice called, "Who are you?"

"I'm Torpid," he called, looking around. "Torpid the Tired."

He heard somebody laugh a pleasant laugh. A red-haired young man, with a harp in one hand, came out of the forest.

"I'm the bard," he said. "I'm practicing this tune, but I can't get it right."

The young bard played, and Torpid listened to every note.

He had heard harp music before, but never like this. It was like listening to the world waking up, or to the best day of your life, or magic. The bard finished his song and held out the harp to Torpid.

"It won't bite," he said. "Try it."

Nervously, Torpid took the small harp. He ran his fingers over the strings, and the sound made him think of bells, and the sea.

"I did that!" he exclaimed. "Wait – how in the world did I do that?"

The bard laughed. "I'll teach you to play," he said. "First, though, I have to go and play for the hermit. Come with me, if you like."

CHAPTER 3

Colors and a Cave

Vapid turned around and around, dizzy with color. Brilliant blue and green, red as bright as jewels, the yellow of sunshine and buttercups, and purple as deep as mystery were in the vats and jars around him.

"Be careful around the purple," the woman called. "It's hard to get and it's expensive."

Vapid had never really looked at colors before. He had always thought of them as "sort of like sunset" or "muddyish." Now he saw bowls of every shade of yellow from cream to golden, every blue from pale sky to midnight, and every red from seashell pink to the deepest burgundy.

"Do you use all these yourself?" he asked. Secretly he was longing to paint a pot or dye a garment, or anything that would give him a chance to play with the colors. "Do you dye cloth?"

"Sure I do," she said, "but these little jars of paint are for the books the old hermit in the cave makes. Most bookmakers have apprentices or somebody to make their paint. As it is, he works in his cave and I send him his colors. The Vikings burned his hut, where he worked before." She looked closely at his helmet. "Speaking of Vikings, what's that on your head?"

Vapid whipped off the helmet, fidgeted with it, and held it out. "It's for you," he said. "You can use it to hold paint."

"That's a funny paint pot," she muttered. "It'll fall over." However, after she stuck it in the ground, it looked as if it could be useful.

"I suppose I should go," Vapid said, though he looked longingly at the paints. "I don't know where my friends are."

"Where did you leave them?"

"Somewhere on the beach." He turned to face her, and wondered where he had put down the spear, and then why she had picked it up. She looked tremendously strong.

He backed away as she advanced toward him, pointing the spear. Staggering back in fear, he tripped over a stone. With a long, fierce stride she was upon him. Before he could move, she had taken his hand and pulled him to his feet.

"I only want you to hold this," she said, "while I get my bits and pieces together."

She strapped a well-loaded basket to her back, and filled another with small pots of paint. She gave one to Vapid, keeping hold of the spear as she did so.

"We'll take this batch to the hermit first," she said. "By the way, my name's Ingy."

"I'm Vapid."

"I thought so. I like this spear," she said, and used it as a walking stick. "Be careful you don't drop that paint."

Torpid followed the bard to the hermit's cave and wondered how much farther it could be. It was hard to keep up, and he was hungry. A nap and something to eat would be good, only he didn't like to ask. He yawned hugely.

"I'm sorry!" the bard called. "Shall we sing? Singing makes the way seem easier."

Torpid liked singing, and was good at it, but the Viking songs were all about thieving and plundering, burning down and pillaging.

In positive songs, they were about escaping in your longship, and in negative songs, about dying in foreign lands. He didn't think he should sing one of those. The bard began to sing about mountains and rivers and the sky and living creatures, and they walked uphill along a path that twisted and narrowed. Then they saw two men sitting at a cave entrance.

Their heads were bent, and they seemed to be drawing with their fingers on the ground. Torpid recognized one of them.

Then there was a sound of slithering, a cry of "help!" and a hail of loose stones that made them all look up. Vapid and Ingy were stumbling and slithering down a cliff path, and Vapid was carrying something in a basket.

"Morbid! Torpid!" he called to them with a broad smile.

"Vapid! Morbid!" Torpid called, waving.

Morbid looked up. "Oh, it's you two," he said, and went back to his drawing.

CHAPTER 4

Ingy the Thingy

"And that's the truth as I learned it many years ago," the bearded old man said. He stood up stiffly to welcome his visitors.

"Good morning, Hermit," Ingy said. "Put the basket in the cave, Vapid, and come and sit down. We'll eat soon."

At the word *eat*, everyone brightened up – even Morbid. Soon they were all seated outside the cave in a circle. Vapid tried to explain that they were, um, sort of warriors, but they weren't very, uh, good at it, and they just sort of turned up here. Ingy stopped him before he could say anything more.

"Eat now, talk later," she said. She took the basket from her back and brought out bread, butter, cheese, cold meat, cold chicken, smoked fish, apples, and jars of cider, and after that nobody said much until they had finished.

"Now," Ingy said, "Hermit lives in a cave and makes books. Bard lives anywhere, and makes music. I live out at the edge of the village – I have to – some of those dyes smell perfectly rotten in summer."

"She's the most important person around here," Bard said. "She's our Helper."

"Wise One," Hermit said.

"Thingy," Ingy said firmly. "Just Thingy, please. Now, what are we to do with the three of you? You can stay here, if you make yourselves useful."

"Can I help you?" Vapid said eagerly. "I could mix things, or fetch things, or…"

"Fall into things," Morbid muttered.

"You can learn to make colors," Ingy said. "Maybe you'll learn to use them too."

"It's no use asking Torpid – he's asleep again," Bard said. "However, I think he wants to learn music."

"That leaves me," Morbid said gruffly. "I know what I want. I don't suppose you'll let me do it, but I'll tell you."

He reached down and drew a zigzag on the ground. "Do you see that? That's *M* for *Morbid* – isn't that amazing? I just learned that! I want to do what Hermit does. I want to read and write."

Hermit smiled a deep smile that he couldn't hide behind his beard.

"My son, listen to my words of instruction," he said. "It's a long time since I had a pupil. One day, you might help me to make books."

"Books?" Morbid suddenly peered down inside his tunic.

"What is he doing?" Ingy asked, but Morbid wasn't listening. With great care he lifted out the treasure they had taken from the town.

"This is a book, isn't it?" he said. "It's the first one I've ever seen."

Hermit's face was as bright as if he'd seen a vision. Joy and pain glowed in his eyes. His old hands trembled as he took the book and, slowly and lovingly, turned its pages.

"Can you read it?" Morbid said eagerly.

"Read it? Read it?" He gave a cry that was half a laugh and half a sob. "I wrote it!"

"Then you should have it back," Morbid said. It wasn't an easy thing to say, but he knew he had to.

"I didn't make it for myself," Hermit said. "I made it for the people of Edwinsbay. Now, I wonder how it came to be hidden in a man's tunic? A man who wears a helmet, and carries a sword and battle-ax?"

Morbid would have lied but Hermit wasn't a person he wanted to lie to, so he and Vapid told their story.

Morbid told the story the short way. Vapid told the story the long way. Torpid simply kept snoring.

"We never wanted to plunder," Vapid said. "We only kept that book because Harald might have burned it if we hadn't hidden it. Oh, we stole a goat, but I don't know what happened to it. I think Harald took it."

"He's probably eaten it by now," Morbid grunted. "I liked that goat. It had a nice face."

"Well, if you're such useless Vikings, you'd better stay here," Ingy said. "Come on, time to go to work! Morbid, get to your reading. Vapid, come with me, and Torpid – oh, can't somebody wake him up?"

So they stayed. They stayed all winter and spring. Morbid worked hard and learned to read all the stories in the book. He became almost happy, and Hermit said he couldn't be "the Miserable" anymore.

Torpid learned to play the harp, sing, and stay awake, all at the same time. He learned the power of a lively tune to stir people up, and a gentle one to bring peace. He learned sad songs that would make people cry, funny ones to make people laugh, and stirring ones to make people bold. Bard said he was a natural musician and should have been making music all his life.

Vapid, under Ingy's instruction, found that he couldn't be vague about paint. It was just about impossible – not to mention completely useless – to say something was "not quite red," or "sort of blue." He had to know his scarlet from his crimson, his indigo from his purple, his egg-yolk yellow from his butter yellow. When he took paint to the cave, Hermit would make him a pen, and he would draw patterns and pictures. He liked that best of all. Sometimes they all forgot they had ever been failed Vikings in longships. It was as if they had always lived with these peaceful people. The spear came in useful for stirring paint, and for playing games on the beach, but nobody ever did any harm with it.

One spring afternoon, when the day's work was finished, the Vikings and Ingy were playing spear-throwing games on the beach. Ingy, who had a powerful arm, was doing extremely well, when Torpid pointed out to sea and said, "What's that?"

A small boat was approaching very slowly. It was still far away, but it looked just like the boat they had arrived in. Three of them had taken turns rowing that boat, but in this one, there was one man. He rowed wearily, as if he had been at sea for a long, long time.

CHAPTER 5

The Story of the Stranger

As the boat drew near, they could see the rower. His helmet looked like a Viking helmet, and there was something familiar about him. Morbid and Vapid waded out to pull the little boat to shore, while Ingy and Torpid started making a fire because, Ingy said, their visitor was probably feeling cold.

The man in the boat was so stiff and chilled they each had to take an arm and heave him out, and his walk rolled from side to side as if he were still at sea. In spite of his helmet, he couldn't be a real Viking. His hair was too short, and so was he. He was beardless, with a dimpled chin.

As they gradually let go of him, the stranger managed to stay upright and not fall over. When he turned to look at Vapid, then Morbid, then Torpid, his face darkened and twitched with rage.

"YOU THREE!" he bellowed. "I SWEAR I
WILL MAKE YOU PAY FOR THIS SOMEHOW,
SOME WAY! EVERYTHING IS YOUR
FAULT, YOU IMBECILES!"

"Oh. Hello, Harald," said Vapid. "I
didn't recognize you without…"

Harald Hairyhand had already grabbed his sword, and it was too late to remember that none of them carried weapons anymore. The blade flashed as he lunged at Torpid. There was a grunt and a thump as Morbid dived at Harald's ankles and tackled him. Ingy then forced him to let go of the sword by tickling him in the armpits. Harald kicked, struggled, threatened, and bellowed, but there were four of them to hold him down – three, when Ingy offered Harald water from a leather bottle and some food from the basket.

By the time Harald had eaten two loaves of bread, a whole chicken, some cheese, a smoked fish, and one more to loaf to finish off, and Torpid had played some soothing music, he was in a slightly better mood. At least he looked as if he wouldn't jump at anyone for awhile.

"The new look suits you," Torpid said. "I like your short hair and no beard." A stone spun through the air, and only missed him because he ducked.

"It is NOT a look!" Harald snarled. "I spent years growing that beautiful beard." He stopped to lick chicken grease from his fingers, then told his story.

"When you feeble runts ruined the raid, you managed to wake the whole countryside.

Next thing you know, we had a war on our hands. I could have raided the whole coastline if it weren't for that, but their reinforcements came from everywhere at once. We ended up on the beach, surrounded on three sides, outnumbered ten to one. The only way we could go was back to the longships."

"So why didn't you get into them?" Morbid asked. "You all could have gone home." He ducked as Harald aimed another pebble at him.

"That's what they all said," Harald snarled, "but I hadn't come all that way for nothing! How would it look when I got home? When Fetid the Foul went raiding, he brought back half a village and a dozen prize boars. What about Rancid the Rotten?"

Rancid the Rotten was the one Viking who was even more feared than Harald. At the mention of his name, all three of the Vikings shuddered.

"Rancid," Harald continued, "carried off enough gold and silver to sink a dragon. On my last expedition, you could have toppled a troll with the gold I brought home! This time, what did I have?"

"A goat," Vapid said helpfully. Harald threw another pebble and everyone ducked except Ingy, who caught it.

"Stop that," she said. "You could put out somebody's eye. So you wanted to gather your men for one more attack, did you?"

"I kept them on the beach that night, ready to attack at dawn. I was on duty for the first watch, then I slept until morning, and when I woke up…"

He was looking at the sand. The faintest shade of pink had crept into the smooth face.

"It wasn't the goat's fault," he muttered. "It's a nice goat, and it was hungry. When I woke up, it had eaten my beard, and most of my hair. I'd been growing that beard since I was fourteen. Even Rancid the Rotten was impressed by that beard. Not a single whisker was left, and there was the goat, with half my ponytail hanging out of its mouth. Worst of all, my men were laughing! Do you hear? LAUGHING AT ME!"

"That's really sad," Morbid said, trying not to look at Vapid.

"Terribly sad," Vapid giggled, and Torpid couldn't say anything because he was rolling on the sand laughing and stuffing his fist in his mouth.

"They wouldn't listen to a word I said, after that," Harald said. "They weren't going to obey me for anything, looking like this.

They were rowing back to Norway before you could say 'pack of puffins'."

"Didn't they even let you go with them?" Ingy asked.

"Do you think I was going to go with them? I had my pride. I stayed on that beach, and when the locals arrived I made the best fight of it I could. You should have seen that fight! Churned was the sand, and piled high with their fallen townspeople..."

"Oh, don't start," Morbid said. He knew Harald wanted to tell a long and exaggerated story with heaps of alliteration like, "Fighting with fury he felled the foe," and, "Proud with his purpose, he panicked the puffins."

"What happened after the fight?" Ingy said.

"They took me prisoner," he sulked. "I should have fought my way out, but they took me prisoner."

"That must have been difficult," Morbid said. "A damp, smelly cell underground, yucky food, no blanket, and things crawling over you in the night."

"It wasn't so bad," Harald said, and for the first time he was more like a Norwegian farmer than a warrior. "The bread wasn't too dry and the blanket wasn't too scratchy.

Really, for a dungeon, it was reasonable. They talked about what they should do to me, but they decided to let me live and repair the damage we'd done. They wouldn't let me grow my hair and beard again, in case I frightened the children," he grumbled.

"I worked hard on the land, and they let me train their horses. I enjoyed it. I used to do all that at home, before I left home to go raiding and pillaging. They're nice people at Edwinsbay, once you stop tormenting them and get to know them. Also, in spite of the trouble it caused me, I liked that goat. I looked after him, and he liked me. He followed me everywhere."

"It was just waiting for his beard to grow again," Morbid muttered, but he made sure Harald didn't hear. Out loud, he only said, "Then what happened?"

"VIKINGS!" Harald exploded. "There we were, a happy, peaceful community minding our own business, and along came all these Viking ships, ready to raid and plunder!"

"That's terrible," Morbid agreed. "There are some horrible people out there."

"Were they any Vikings in particular?" Vapid asked.

"Rancid," Harald muttered, to gasps of terror from all around the fire. "I'm surprised you can't catch a whiff of him from here."

"They say the smell of Rancid the Rotten can kill a puffin at twenty paces," Torpid shuddered. "He's always plundering and never washes his hands afterward. I've heard it said that his feet are stuck to his sandals."

"I did my best," said Harald, "I fought to save Edwinsbay, but Rancid's men caught me and cast me off to sea in that leaky little tub. The worst of it is that Rancid and his men didn't just raid the village and go. They've taken over and have forced the local people to work for them. They intend to stay."

At the thought of the kind, gentle people of Edwinsbay being ruled by Rancid the Rotten, everybody fell into glum silence. Well, at least almost everybody did.

Not Ingy, though. She stomped across the sand and came back, dragging a boat from a cave.

"Good thing I repaired this," she said.

"Haven't I seen that boat before?" Vapid asked warily.

"It's ours!" said Torpid. "We rowed all the way here in that."

"Who did?" Morbid muttered. "You were asleep, if I remember correctly."

"I don't understand," Vapid said. "Have I missed something? Why do we need the boat again?"

"Because," Harald explained, "we're not going to let Rancid the Rotten treat all those wonderful people like slaves, are we, troll-face? We have to go there and throw out Rancid and his men. It will be hard, but that isn't the point."

"We'll be destroyed," Morbid said, "but that isn't the point either. We have to do it."

CHAPTER 6

The Return of the Vikings

"We'll arm ourselves before we go," said Harald. "Swords and battle-axes all around."

"You won't need them," Ingy said. "You can have this old spear if you like." Harald took the spear and inspected it.

"This was a fine spear before you three got ahold of it," he said. "It's blunt now. Four of us, and a blunt spear, to take on Rancid the Rotten and all his Vikings. You're all useless fighters too."

"Excuse me, who said anything about fighting?" Ingy asked.

Morbid scowled. "Rancid won't leave just because we ask him nicely," he said.

"Yes, but there are only four of you, and three of you can't fight," Ingy said. "What do you think your brains are for?"

The three Vikings said a quick, sad, and difficult good-bye to Hermit, Bard, and Ingy.

Vapid had some dyes to take with him, and Torpid had his own harp and his whistle, and Morbid had a quill and ink and a piece of parchment. To his great joy, Hermit gave him the book, saying that because it came from Edwinsbay, it should be returned there.

At last, Ingy shoved the boat into the water. It bobbed and rocked, and they were on their way. Then Vapid remembered that he had left his helmet upside down and full of orange dye, but it was too late to go back.

Torpid raised his sword over the cowering figure of Rancid the Rotten and with all his might yelled, "Surrender!" The sword in his hands turned into a puffin that twisted around to look at him. Rancid sprang up with a fish in each hand . . .

Torpid, as usual, was dreaming. He woke as Morbid sloshed water in his face.

"Wake up, useless," Morbid was saying. "Land in sight."

Torpid yawned enormously, stretched, and sat up. He was wet and cold and didn't feel much like facing anyone, let alone Rancid.

"This isn't where we landed," he said.

"Not exactly," said Vapid.

"Of course it isn't," Harald said. "We're not steering for the bay, you imbecile brigade. Rancid will have lookouts all over the place.

We're heading for the south side, and the cave where you found this boat. Then we'll scope the layout of the land and see what we can do."

"Capture Rancid and all his men and set the people free," Morbid said. "Easy peasy, the goat smells cheesy."

"Rumble mumble, Morbid's a grumble," Torpid sang.

"I wish I knew what happened to the goat," Harald said sadly, as they brought the boat up to the beach. "I called him Eric. I hope Rancid hasn't eaten him."

"Don't worry too much, Harald," Torpid said as they stretched their cramped legs and walked around the sand. "We'll find him."

They heaved the boat into the cave where they had first found it. The sun was high, and Harald suggested they should stay out of the way until evening.

"That's when the Vikings all sit around the fire, gorge on food, and tell terrific tall tales about their battles," Harald explained.

"There are guards on duty, but they're usually so full of food, they're asleep too."

So they stayed in the cave where Torpid played his harp very quietly, and Morbid opened his book and read stories, and Vapid drew patterns on the ground with a sharp stick, and Harald talked about the good times he'd had among these people before Rancid the Rotten came.

As the afternoon dragged on they talked less and less, and looked out at the fading light. Torpid played the wrong notes because he couldn't concentrate, Morbid lost his place in his book, and Vapid gave up drawing anything. At last Harald said it was dark enough to creep out and do some spying.

"I can't see a thing," Vapid muttered.

"Be quiet and remember your Viking training," said Harald.

They slipped out in single file, and stood back to look at the top of the cliffs. A fire was burning low, glowing darkly as if it were going out. This, Harald said, was a good sign.

"It means the guards are neglecting it," he said, "so they're probably sound asleep. I'll climb up there and take a look, and wave if it's safe to come up."

"No, I'll do it," Torpid said quickly.

"You?" Harald exclaimed. "But you're…"

"Useless, yes, I know," Torpid whispered. "This way, if I get caught, it's no great loss. We need you, Harald. You're the leader."

"I'll go behind you," Morbid said, "in case you fall off."

Torpid scanned the cliff and said that falling off was something he'd rather not think about, thank you. Harald protested again, but Torpid and Morbid were already scrambling up the cliff side. The two

Vikings felt for footholds in the dark, not daring to look down at the sea.

Step by step, never knowing if the next handhold would be safe, they inched their way up, and slowly, breath by breath and struggle by struggle, they climbed until they hauled themselves over the top of the cliff, where two guards snored by the fire. Far away, they could hear the singing of the Viking troops. It was loud, flat, and very bad. Not a single guard was awake. Morbid waved to the others to join them.

"You're still awake!" Vapid whispered in surprise, as Torpid pulled him up.

"This is too exciting to sleep through!" Torpid said. They lay flat on the grass and looked at the huts, the church, the dying guard fires, and the pens full of animals.

"Now what?" Vapid said.

"That's Rancid's hut, the biggest one," Harald whispered. "The one with the..." He stopped. He was staring at something.

"With the what?" Torpid asked.

"The one," Harald continued, with a tremble in his voice, "with the goat tied up outside it. That's not any old goat, either. It's Eric!"

CHAPTER 7

The Revenge of Harald Hairyhand

Morbid grabbed at Harald's tunic, but it was too late. He was running to the hut where the goat stood tethered. He put his arms around its neck, and it bleated a welcome.

The guards rolled over. One propped himself on his elbow. Torpid, Morbid, and Vapid tried not to breathe. The half-awake guard yawned noisily.

"It's just that goat," he said.

"What goat?" the other mumbled.

"Tomorrow's dinner," the first said, and fell back to sleep.

They waited until the steady rumble of snoring told them that the guards were well and truly asleep again. Then they crawled like snakes to the hut.

There was no goat, and no Harald.

Vapid, still flat on the grass, turned his head enough to whisper, "Didn't anyone see them go?"

"We were all keeping our heads down," Morbid said. "I couldn't see a thing. I guess he's been caught."

"We would have heard something," Vapid pointed out.

Torpid agreed. "There'd have been a fight, or a yell. They'd have made a noise, like you do when you're getting caught by a Viking."

From the darkness came a muffled bleat. They all started.

"It came from that way," Vapid said. "No, that way... no..."

"Shut up and listen!" Torpid whispered. The goat bleated again, a sort of muffled complaint as if someone were trying to keep its mouth shut. Then there was silence. It was a long, dark, and frightening silence.

When the goat bleated again, it was in Morbid's right ear. It was followed by a quick, sharp whisper from Harald: "Come behind the hut and be quiet!" Hushed as it was, there was a note of triumph in his voice.

Swiftly they followed him and huddled behind the hut, where the goat tried to bleat and eat Morbid's tunic at the same time.

"He did it!" Harald whispered, with his arms around the goat. "He did it!"

"Did what?" Torpid said sleepily.

"What he likes doing," Harald explained. "I knew he would! I took him in the hut while Rancid was asleep, and he ate his beard! Every bit, and most of his hair too!"

"Oh, good," Torpid said, rubbing his eyes.

"Don't you bozos get it?" Harald said. "When he did that to me, my men wouldn't follow me anymore. Now Rancid's men won't follow him either! Rancid is in real trouble, and it's all thanks to Eric!"

Vapid and Torpid tried to cheer without making a noise. Morbid shook his head.

"It's not enough," he said. "His men might refuse to follow him, but they'll just choose a new leader and stay here. Your men took to the boats and rowed away, but they already wanted to go. Rancid's men don't."

"Can't we sort of *make* them want to go?" Vapid said. "Scare them off or something?"

"Vikings don't scare easily," Harald said.

"I do," Vapid said, but they ignored him.

"We've got to find something," Morbid said. "Something that makes them so terrified they'll go running back to their ships like lemmings."

Poor Torpid was now fast asleep. Vapid was gazing up at the stars and wondering which ones were which. Harald was a true Viking warrior, but he was short and beardless and didn't look scary. Neither did Morbid.

"Think," Morbid said. "Everybody's frightened of something. What are these Vikings frightened of?"

Then Harald and Morbid grinned at each other. They had both thought of an answer.

"Come on, Vapid," Harald said. "Oh, and wake up Torpid. We need him."

Dawn came overcast and cold over the village. The rooster crowed, coughed, and went back to sleep.

It woke the men and women who faced another day of working for the Vikings. It woke the children, who supposed that today would be all work and no play, as usual, with not enough to eat because Rancid's men ate most of the food. It woke Rancid the Rotten, who sat up, feeling something was wrong, but not knowing exactly what.

It woke Rancid's Vikings, bleary-eyed after a night of sleeping on the ground with rocks for pillows, and ready to take out their foul temper on the local people. In the early half-light, they staggered out of their huts.

What they saw and heard made the blood chill in their veins, and the hair prickle like frost on their arms. Every face turned pale.

A song rose into the air. It was a loud, mysterious wail of a song, like a dirge of death or the moaning of the north wind, long, slow, and fearsome.

These Vikings never feared any living creature. They feared death and anything associated with it.

In the gray early morning they saw a figure standing on the raised ground above Rancid's hut. Everything about him was as pale as ashes, his clothes, his face, the spear in his hand, and even the goat he led by a length of rope. They knew that short figure.

They knew the thick boots, the beardless face, and the shorn hair. They remembered how Harald Hairyhand had been sent away in a small boat. They also knew that the goat – the very goat they were to slaughter today – was Harald's goat. They whispered to each other.

"Harald Hairyhand has come back from the sea…"

"…from the grave…"

"He has come for his enemy."

"He has come for his revenge."

"He has come for his goat."

The figure advanced very, very slowly. Rancid's men shuffled back.

At that moment, Rancid the Rotten staggered from his hut, a spear in his hand.

"What are you idiots staring at?" he growled. "Move yourselves, or I'll whack whoever's nearest over the head!"

At the sight of him, another murmur of dismay ran through the terrified Vikings. The terrible ghost on the hill had stolen the beard of Rancid the Rotten.

"It will take all our beards," someone whispered. They shrank back, step by step.

In the damp, misty morning air, Rancid felt strangely cold. He didn't normally notice a draft around the back of his neck and his chin…

He put up his hand and found a stubbly, pimply space where his beard had been.

"STOP STARING AT ME!" he bellowed.

"We're not staring at you, sir," stammered one of his men, pointing a trembling finger.

For the first time, Rancid heard the mournful singing and the bleating of a goat. He turned around.

At the sight of the ghostly figure, the strength drained out of Rancid as if he were boneless. If he had been alone, he would have turned and run, or hidden under his shield, but he didn't want to look like a coward in front of his men.

"To the longships! To the longships!" the Vikings muttered to each other.

"Stay, you idiots!" Rancid roared. "You weak, scared, pathetic little puffins! One simple ghost can't hurt you!"

At any other time, they would have obeyed him, but not now. No leader could protect them from a ghost, especially this nearly bald leader with the pimply chin.

Rancid made one last attempt. He launched his spear at the figure as it walked steadily toward him.

It was a spear throw that would have killed any living man. It hit the ghost, and bounced off. At the sight of the ghost stepping over the spear, still advancing, every single warrior turned and fled to the longships. The villagers let them go. They were closing in around Rancid as he knelt quivering on the ground.

From their shelter behind the hut, Torpid, Vapid, and Morbid looked out.

"You can stop wailing now, Torpid," Morbid said.

"I thought my song was pretty good," Torpid said indignantly. "It's an ancient lament for the dead. Are they gone yet?"

"Harald's going to stay there until they're well out of the way," Vapid said. "What shall we do about Rancid? Do you think we should sort of rescue him? I mean, I know he's Rancid the Rotten, but he's a Viking and we're still sort of Vikings."

"I don't think these villagers will do him any harm," Torpid said with a yawn. "Harald says they're peace-loving people. I don't suppose they'll do anything too awful to him – except wash him."

This, they agreed, was probably the worst thing that could happen to Rancid the Rotten. Torpid complained about being up half the night, and then fell asleep.

When the longships were out of sight, Harald stopped being a ghost and came to join them and wash the paint and ashes off his face. "Well done, all of us!" he said.

"I used up the white paint on his face," Vapid said. "Frankly, finishing him off with ashes worked rather well."

"It's a good thing you thought of swapping the spears," Harald said to Morbid. He was carrying Rancid's own spear, which he had taken in the night, leaving the blunt one in its place. "That old one nearly knocked me over, but it didn't do me any harm. I wonder how Rancid's doing?"

"I'd go and find out," Morbid said, "but I still look like a Viking. The villagers might capture me too."

"Leave it to me," Harald said. "I'm their friend, remember?"

Everybody from the village seemed to be hurrying to the beach. Harald ran after them crying out that he was their old friend, Harald Hairyhand, and very much alive.

They greeted him with delight as he explained who his friends were and how they had defeated Rancid and scared away Rancid's Vikings.

Torpid, Morbid, and Vapid suddenly found themselves lifted shoulder-high, carried down to the beach, and invited to be honored guests at The Washing of Rancid.

As everyone gathered to watch, Rancid was led into the sea and washed and washed and washed, until his clothes finally unstuck themselves from his body.

They scrubbed him until he changed color, and so did the sea. They washed the scum from his head and the bugs from his tunic and the grime from between his toes. They washed out the mushrooms growing in his sandals. They washed out the tangles in his chest hair, and a few large caterpillars floated away from behind his ears.

When he was as smooth and pink as a bathed baby, they dried him and put him in clean clothes, and he curled up on the sand, biting his nails and whimpering.

"Poor thing," Vapid said. "Now what should we do with him?"

"Ingy would know," Morbid said. "She'd straighten him out in no time."

"Ingy the Thingy?" said a woman in the crowd. "Do you know her?"

It turned out that Ingy was well known to the people of Edwinsbay. Several of them offered to take Rancid and hand him over to her. So he was tied up and put in a boat, and taken along the coast to Ingy's Bay.

For the rest of their lives, the Vikings stayed happily in Edwinsbay. Torpid became their Bard, and Vapid taught them to make dyes and paints, and to use them.

Morbid, of course, returned their book to them, and he and Vapid kept on making beautiful new books.

They all married and had children and grew to be old, but they went on with their music and their books and their paintings to the end of their days.

Harald kept horses and goats and a tame puffin, and was very happy. In addition to becoming the best horse trainer for miles around, he became famous as a goatkeeper. Eric followed him everywhere, nibbling lovingly at his tunic.

Rancid the Rotten never fully recovered from being washed. He became Ingy's helper, and promised to obey her faithfully as long as he didn't have to wash more than once a year. He was very strong, and made himself useful chopping wood and building houses and moving boulders and plowing fields with his bare hands.

When Morbid was old, he decided to write down their story in a book. Unfortunately, he was so very old that he sometimes forgot things, and became confused, and didn't always remember events exactly the way they happened.

Besides, his handwriting was getting wobbly, and the people who copied his book couldn't be sure if they'd gotten it right.

So that is the story of Morbid, Torpid, Vapid, and Harald Hairyhand, as Morbid told it. But is that really how it happened?

What do you think?

About the Author

This book owes everything to my husband, Tony. Long ago, during a very silly conversation, he invented three people whose names were Torpid, Vapid, and Morbid. We agreed that they were Vikings, but not very good ones, and this story grew, very slowly, from there.

Tony and I have spent much of our lives on the northeast coast of England. The closest thing to Vikings we ever met are our dear Norwegian friends. I hope they like this book.

Margaret McAllister